AUTORE

Paolo Crippa (23 April 1978) has cultivated his passion for Italian history since high school. His research interests are focused mainly in the field of military history and in particular on italian armored units from the 30s until the end of World War II. In 2006 he published his first volume, "I Reparti Corazzati della Repubblica Sociale Italiana 1943/1945", the first organic research carried out and published in Italy on the subject. In 2007 he published "Duecento Volti della R.S.I." and in 2011 " Un anno con il 27° Reggimento Artiglieria Legnano". He regularly contributes to several journals: Milites, New Historica, SGM - World War II, Batailes & Blindes, Armoured Vehicles and history of the twentieth century, Mezzi Corazzati, both as an author, or in collaboration with other researchers. He published with the editor Mattioli 1885 in 2014 "Italy 43 – 45 – Civil War improvised AFV's" (2014), "Italian AFV's of the Civil War 1943 - 1945" (2015) and "Italy 43 – 45 – AFV's and MV's of co-belligerent units" (2018).

ACKNOWLEDGMENTS

I would like to thank some people who have made possible to write this volume, contributing in various ways with documents, photographs and testimonies. In strict alphabetical order, the lost cavalier Nino Arena, Carlo Cucut, Andrea Lombardi, Eugenio Vendrame and Carlo Venditti. Finally, I would like to mention the Lieutenant Elvezio Borgatti of the "M" Armored Group "Leonessa", to whose memory I dedicate my work. He was one of the first people to spur me on to deepen my historical research and that prompted me to publish my first volume, giving me many of the photos in this book, as well as lots of Group documents. In his company I spent pleasant moments, enriched by his long and moving stories, living testimony of his experience in the "M" "Leonessa" Group.

For a complete list of Soldiershop titles please contact Luca Cristini Editore on our website: www.soldiershop.com or www.cristinieditore.com. E-mail: info@soldiershop.com

Titolo: **THE TANKERS OF MUSSOLINI** Code.: **WTW-003 GB**
by Paolo Crippa.
ISBN code: 978-88-93274579 first edition May 2019
Text: English Nr. of images 100 layout: 177,8x254mm Cover & Art Design: Luca S. Cristini

WITNESS TO WAR (SOLDIERSHOP) is a trademark of Luca Cristini Editore, via Orio, 35/4 - 24050 Zanica (BG) ITALY.

WITNESS TO WAR

THE TANKERS
OF MUSSOLINI

ARMOURED GROUP "LEONESSA" FROM M.V.S.N. TO R.S.I

PHOTOS & IMAGES FROM WORLD WARTIME ARCHIVES

PAOLO CRIPPA

ENGLISH TEXT

SOLDIERSHOP
PUBLISHING

BOOKS TO COLLECT

CONTENTS

▲ Title page of a publication published by the Command of the XV Legion of the Militia of Brescia, to celebrate the heroic deeds performed by the Black Shirts of Brescia in the land of Russia. Along with the Mussolini with the beam, the emblem of the city of Brescia, "Lioness of Italy" is also drawn.

THE TANKERS OF MUSSOLINI

"M" BATTALIONS GROUP "LEONESSA"

The 15th Black Shirts Battalion of Brescia came from the XV Legion of Brescia, called "Leonessa" in honor of its city, called "Leonessa of Italy". Framed with the XIV Battalion of Bergamo in the 114th Black Shirts Legion "Garibaldina" participated at the Ethiopian Campaign, in the "23rd October" Division.

After the outbreak of the Second World War the "Brescia" Battalion was sent on the Greek-Albanian front, forming, with the "Bergamo" Battalion, the Black Shirts Legion "Leonessa". On October 1st, 1941 the officers, non-commissioned officers and legionaries of the "Leonessa" Legion were awarded the red "M" as a badge of honor for their behavior during the war campaigns in which they had been engaged. The "Leonessa" Black Shirt Battalion Group, part the Voluntary National Security Militia (M.V.S.N.), with about 1,800 men, was established on 1st January 1942 under the command of Consul Graziano Sardu. The "Leonessa" was formed by the XIV Black Shirts Battalion of Bergamo, from the XV Black Shirts Battalion of Brescia and from the XXXVIII Light Weapons Battalion of Asti. Together with the Black Shirts Legion "Valle Scrivia" was assigned to the Russian Front on 26th June 1942, reaching its own area of operations in July, but not arriving in time to participate in the First Battle of the Don. On December 13th the "Leonessa" Group arrived in Orobinski. just 3 km away from the Don River; the next morning the "Leonessa" launched an attack to the positions held by the Russians at Quote 192, positions that had been lost by the 90th Infantry Regiment "Cosseria". The fight was particularly bloody, the Seniore Comincioli, commander of the XV "Leonessa" Battalion, 8 officers and about twenty legionaries fell, the number of wounded and missing exceeded 220 units. On the 15th the defensive line was kept at the cost of serious sacrifices, the "Leonessa" continued to withstand the shock of the Russian troops until the 17th, when, on German order, it began to fall back towards Mitrofanovka, but ended up surrounded by Zapkovo. Galvanized by the incessant presence of the console commander Sardu, the Black Shirts managed to break through the encirclement, thanks to the decisive intervention of German armored vehicles and to finally reach Mitrofanovka.

The remains of the "Leonessa", about 550 men, were sent to the defense of the Donez river and from 21st January 1943 they began to fall back first to the rear and then to Italy on 17th March.

1st LEGIONARY ARMORED DIVISON "M"

At the beginning of April 1943, during a meeting between Carlo Scorza, secretary of the National Fascist Party, and Heinrich Himmler, a project dating back to 1942 was dusted off, which aimed to constitute a Division faithful to the Duce, modernly armed and placed in its direct dependencies, ready to intervene in the event of unrest against the fascist regime. Mussolini therefore accepted Himmler's offer for the supply of Germanic means and instructors for the establishment of the 1st Armored Division Black Shirts "M". In the meantime, the survivors of the Russian front of the "Leonessa" Group were gathered at the gates of Rome, while legionaries of the "M" Battalions, distinguished in the fighting and coming from other fronts, also flocked simultaneously. An important problem appeared immediately during the establishment of the Division: the Militia could only supply infantry departments, not having specialized personnel. The Division, which Mussolini never conceived as a personal guard, was initially deployed near Chiusi (SI), a location chosen only for logistical and non-tactical reasons and was officially established on March 23rd, 1943. At the end of June, the Division was moved on Lake Bracciano in Campagnano Romano (near Rome). The Germans supplied modern material, but not enough to constitute a true Armored Division: in fact, the Division received 12 Panzer IV Ausf. G, 12 Panzer III Ausf. N and 12 Sturmgeschütz III Ausf. G, who were placed in the Tanks Group "Leonessa", on three Companies, under the command of the 1st Senior Ferdinando Tesi. The troops of the Tanks Group came largely from the Black Shirts Group "Leonessa", which had fought in Russia as an infantry unit. To obviate the lack of experience in driving and maintaining the armored vehicles of the Black Shirts, about fifty tank crews from the Royal Army were temporarily attached to the Division, who were to assist the German instructors. The Division also received 24 88/56 guns, useful for both the anti-aircraft and anti-tank fire, with their semi-tracked tractors, which equipped the "Valle Scrivia" Artillery Group on two Groups of 3 Batteries each.

However, the formation of the great unit proceeded slowly due to the open distrust of the Army General Staff, which considered it a possible threat. On 10th July an exercise was organized in the presence of the Duce; to mask the poor level of preparation of the specialists, only 9 armored vehicles were used, 3 for each model supplied with the Division, moreover driven by German instructors, and only one Artillery Battery. Mussolini was enthusiastic about this demonstration, so much so that he proposed to launch the Division against the Allies, which had just landed in Sicily, as soon as possible, but the departure from Rome, fortunately, there was not, thus avoiding sending this unit still in constitution to the fray.

On 25th July 1943 the Duce was dismissed during the session of the Grand Council of Fascism and the consequences for this Division with a strong political connotation were not slow to arrive: by the General Command of M.V.S.N. came the order to maintain positions, displeasing most of the legionaries, who wished to move against the capital. In the following days the Militia made itself available to the Badoglio government, which ordered to remove from the uniforms and vehicles all the symbols that recalled Fascism. The black shirts were therefore replaced by the gray-green ones, the black fezzes disappeared in favor of the Army caps and the lapel stars took the place of red bundles and "M".

On 26th July, the commander of the Division General Console Armando Luserna was replaced by General Giorgio Calvi di Bergolo (son-in-law of the king and therefore considered "reliable"), already commander of the "Centauro" Armored Division on the Libyan front. The Division had to change its name to 136th Armored Legionary Division "Centaur II" and was also removed from the capital, split into a vast area east of Rome, with the order to continue training, which proceeded much more quickly thanks to the new directives given by General Calvi di Bergolo.

To further empty the "fascist" soul of the Great Unit, a circular dated 24th August sanctioned the constitution of the 131st Tanks Battalion, composed by the Tanks Group "Leonessa" and from the XIX Tanks Battalion of the Royal Army, stationed in Piombino (LI), which never reached the Division though.

The Armistice of 8th September produced a great impression in the units of the Division. On the morning of the 9th the order came to fall back to Tivoli, to block the Via Tiburtina from any German infiltration in the capital, but the situation became increasingly confused with the passing of the hours, while the unitts moved in an uncoordinated manner. The news of the "ceasefire" agreement signed between the Italian military commanders of Rome and the German troops arrived the next day. The Division remained on its positions, uncertain as to what to do, and in the afternoon, it received the order to disarm and to hand over all the materials to the Germans, a fact which, together with the arrival of the news of the liberation of Mussolini to the Gran Sasso, marked the definitive collapse of the Division. Some of the staff abandoned the position, others tried to stay, in that atmosphere of confusion that characterized those terrible days. On 13th September weapons and armor were concentrated and taken over by the German paratroopers of the 2.Fallschirmjäger Division. It was the end of the 1st Legionary Armored Division "M", but three officers and sixty legionaries decided to continue the war alongside the now ex-German allies.

STRUCTURE

The organization chart for the Division was as follows:

- Command and Command Company
- Carabinieri's Company (Military Police)
- • Road Movement Nucleus (Milizia della Strada)
- 306° Military Post Office
- Divisional Car Department
- Tanks Group "M" "Leonessa":

    1st Tanks Company on 4 Platoons (with Panzer IV Ausf. G)

    2nd Tanks Company on 4 Platoons (with Panzer III Ausf. N)

    3rd Self Propelled Guns Company on 4 Platoons (with Sturmgeschütz III Ausf. G)

- Battalions Group "M" "Tagliamento"
- LXIII "M" Assault Battalion
- LXXIX "M" Assault Battalion
- XLI "M" Light Weapons Battalion "Montebello"
- VI "M" Assault Battalion
- XXX "M" Assault Battalion
- XII "M" Light Weapons Battalion
- "M" Artillery Group "Valle Scrivia":

    1st Group on 3 Batteries

    2nd Group on 3 Batteries

- Sappers Battalion
- Mixed Engineers Units:

    Engineers Company

    Telegraphists Company

    1st Radio Telegraphists Company

    2nd Radio Telegraphists Company

- Military Health Care Nucleus
- Subsistence Nucleus
- Commissioner Office

▲ The XV Battalion Black Shirts "Leonessa" of Brescia, reviewed in the city on August 17th, 1936, returning from the victorious campaign in Ethiopia.

▼ Legionaries of the Voluntary National Security Militia leaving for the Russian front.

▲ The XV Battalion Black Shirts "M" of Brescia of the Legion of Assault "Lioness" lined up completely before the departure for Russia, under the command of the elderly Comincioli.

▶ Seniore Giacomo Comincioli fell on 15th December 1942 near Orobinskji, an action for which he was decorated with the fourth Silver Medal for Military Valor. On the lapel, above the black flames of the Militia, you can see the red "M", a badge of honor granted to the Battalion on 1st October 1941.

▲ Group of tanker legionaries facing their own Panzer III. The military wear the common blue overalls, distributed to all the crews of the Regio Esercito floats, with the black fez of M.V.S.N. (Arena).

▼ A Panzer III Ausf. N with the insignia of the Armored Group "Leonessa", framed in the 1st Armored Division CC.NN. "M" (Arena).

▲ The Panzer III Ausf. N represented the latest version of this family of tried and tested armored vehicles, which constituted the backbone of all German armored units (Arena) .

▼ Panzer IV Ausf. G of the CC.NN. Armored Division "M" marching during training (Arena).

▲ The same tabk of the previous photograph is about to overcome a stretch of bush (Arena).

▲ Black shirts of the Armored Division "M" quickly climbing aboard their self-propelled (Arena).

◄ Contrary to what one might believe, the Germans provided Italy with the best they had in terms of armored vehicles. The Panzer IV, with its 7.5 L/48 cannon, was at that time one of the best German tanks, outclassed only later by the Panther (Arena).

▲ Platoon of Sturmgeschütz III Ausf. G of the 3rd Company of the Armored Group "Leonessa" in a moment of rest (Arena).

▼ July 25th marked the end of the Mussolini parable and also the vehicles of the "M" Division suffered a "maquillage": the emblem with the red "M" appearing on the side of this StuG will in fact be canceled with strokes of paint (Arena).

▲ Close up of a StuG III of the "Leonessa" with a Panzer IV of the same Group behind it. The photo shows the coat of arms painted on the saddle of the self-propelled and formed by a blue rhombus edged in black and loaded with the Mussolinian monogram (Arena).

▲ The frantic days that followed September 8th 1943 threw the country into chaos. In the capital, two tanks of the "Leonessa" arrive in Piazza Colonna: the tankers wear a black shirt again (Crippa).

R.S.I.'s "M" ARMORED GROUP "LEONESSA"

On September 21st, 1943, faced with the collapse followed by the Armistice, a group of officers and legionaries of the 1st Legionary Armored Division "M", mostly tank crews, concentrated at the "Mussolini" barracks in Rome, took the resolution to rebuild the dissolved Group "Leonessa", with the intention of continuing the war alongside the German Armed Forces. The staff of M.V.S.N., that on September 8th had put again the red "M" and the black shirts on, refusing the Armistice, had remained on foot and was forced to look for weapons and materials in the now empty Italian barracks. In Rome some vehicles and two M tanks, used then to guard the headquarters of the EIAR (Italian Radio) and the direction of the reborn Fascist Party in Piazza Colonna, were thus recovered at the Tiburtino Fort, headquarters and depot of the 4th Tanks Regiment[1].

On 29th September the newborn unit was transferred to the province of Brescia, to Montichiari; the men reached the north by train, along with the few vehicles recovered in Rome. Here the legionaries were subjected to an intense training cycle, while the ranks of the unit began to grow rich with volunteers from all over the territory of the R.S.I. and the cadres of the officers were gradually reinforced both with a good number of men from the dissolved Royal Army and, later on, with sub-lieutenants of the Officers Schools of the Republican National Guard. In Montichiari the Group Command was immediately established, together with the 1st Company, followed shortly thereafter by the 2nd Company.

Meanwhile, October 4th, the commander general of the reborn M.V.S.N. General Renato Ricci, issued a statement decreeing the reconstitution of the dissolved Division M: "*I have ordered that the 1st Armored Division" M" have to be immediately reconstituted. Therefore, all officers, non-commissioned officers and legionaries already belonging to the Division itself and those wishing to be incorporated there, were invited to report to the Militia Mobilization Center closest to their residence* ". The Consul General Lusana was in charge of the command of the unit, of which the Senior Cioni was the Chief of Staff. Until October 15th, the "Leonessa" Group was commanded by the First Senior (Lieutenant Colonel) Ferdinando Tesi, who however took on an important position at the Ministry of the Economy. On that date the command passed to the vice commander, Senior (Major) Priamo Swich, who was later promoted to Lieutenant Colonel.

Initially the unit was almost devoid of armored vehicles and, for this reason, at the end of October 1943 the General Command of G.N.R. (then again M.V.S.N.[2]) advanced the hypothesis of transforming the "Leonessa" into a Public Order Battalion. In fact, General Ricci reported to the officers, communicating the decision to transform the "Leonessa" into a non-armored unit due to the lack of armored vehicles, following the fate of many other units of the Republican National Guard. Ricci pointed out that the difficult internal situation, following the disastrous 8th September, made it impossible to reconstitute armored units; it was also necessary to organize units that could intervene to restore order to those areas where the phenomenon of stragglers was giving rise to forms of banditry. The determined and insistent reaction of Swich and the officers of the Group, who promised to go in search of the tanks needed, caused the commander of the GNR, moved and impressed by the firmness of these men, not to carry out the dissolution order, granting two months to form the armored department.

---

[1] Lieutenant General Montagna, commander of the Militia since 17th September, stated that he had recovered forty tanks in Rome in good condition, which had been abandoned by the Italian armored troops during the fighting in the capital, following the Armistice.

[2] The Republican National Guard was officially born with the Law Decree of Duce No. 913 of December 24th, 1943. It was formed by M.V.S.N. (of which the "Leonessa" Group was a part), by the Carabinieri and by the Italian Africa Police. The G.N.R. became part of the Republican National Army, as the first combat unit, on 14th August 1944 with Decree Law 469.

Thus, began an intense search and recovery activity for armored vehicles for the Group. Some officers organized an impressive information and patrol service at the tanks's depots of Norther Italy (Bologna, Vercelli, Verona, Siena in particular) and at the Ansaldo and FIAT factories to find and recover abandoned armored vehicles to be used by the Group. The results were satisfactory, were soon assembled some tanks, several trucks, fuel reserves, weapons and equipment. Many armored vehicles were also found hidden in the countryside, where they had been left by the crews that had no orders at the Armistice. Two Lieutenants, both coming from the dissolved Royal Army, Loffredo Loffredi and Giovanni Ferraris, distinguished themselves particularly in this recovery activity. The work of fine-tuning the armored vehicles was particularly demanding and for this reason a Workshop for the Group was organized, under the supervision of Lieutenant Soncini, assisted by Lieutenant Dente, who, thanks to the tenacity of the specialists, was able to make available to the Group the vehicles in a short time, putting back in order also vehicles that were in desperate conditions. At the end of December, the "Leonessa" could begin training on the vehicles. The staff of the Group began to grow rich with volunteers from all over the territory of the R.S.I. and the cadres of the officers were gradually reinforced both by officers from the dissolved Royal Army and, later on, by Second Lieutenants of the Officers School of the Republican National Guard.

On December 15th, meanwhile, the Armored Division CC.NN. "M" was officially dissolved and with it all the departments that constituted it, with the exception of the Armored Group "Leonessa", of the XXX Black Shirts Battalion "Montebello" and of the LXIII Black Shirts Battalion "Tagliamento".

During the period of stay in Montichiari the Group not only followed the training cycle necessary for an armored unit, but also carried out some police actions and managed to capture several British prisoners of war, who had fled the prison camps due to the state of confusion created by the Armistice. On February 9th, 1944, finally, the "Leonessa" could swear allegiance to the Italian Social Republic in Piazza della Vittoria in Brescia, along with other departments of the G.N.R., and, on this occasion, paraded for the first time in the streets of the city applauded by the crowd, completely motorized and with a fair number of armored vehicles. General Ricci, commander of the G.N.R., was positively impressed and, to express his satisfaction, he received a representation of legionaries and non-commissioned officers at the General Command, declaring that he had personally verified that the Group was now fit for combat. Meanwhile, the General Command of G.N.R. planned to set up his own Division, in which to frame many autonomous departments. This was called the 1st Antiparachutist and Tankhunter Division of the G.N.R. "Etna" and the Armored Group "Leonessa" became part of it, moving into the employ of the newly formed Division the following August.

In a note for the Duce, dated March 1st, 1944, we read that "[...] *the armored group of the GNR, of the strength of a Battalion, composed of a Tank Company, an Truck Company, an Engineers Company, is located in Montichiari in training. The instructors are German* ". In fact, the Group was part of G.N.R., but it was available for use by the Hocster SS[3].

With the intervention of Ricci, the Group became operational. The legionaries had lulled themselves in the hope of being able to be sent to the front, but their destination was another. In fact, on March 5th the headquarters of the Group was transferred to Turin, as a reinforcement for the Provincial Command of the National Guard, and was destined to operate against the partisan bands in Piedmont. The departure of the "Leonessa" from Montichiari was celebrated with a moving ceremony, during which the town's fascist women offered the fighting pennant to the Group. The two Companies of the "Leonessa" carried out activities mainly anti-partisan in Piedmont and Lombardy. In these two regions the Group established numerous small operational detachments, often equipped with only one or two

3   Chief of SS and Police in Italy.

armored vehicles, guaranteeing a widespread presence that allowed them to preside over the areas considered most at risk and the most important military and industrial installations. The "Leonessa" also participated in large-scale operations, such as the liberation of Alba, Val d'Ossola, the "Nachtigal Operation" in the Germinasca and Pellice Valleys. Another activity of fundamental importance carried out by the armored vehicles of the Group was the constant patrolling of the Milan-Turin motorway, a major road junction, which connected the real capital of the Social Republic with the most important industrial center in Northern Italy.

Constant was the influx of new legionaries along the twenty months of the "Leonessa", the youngest came from the White Flames, the newly appointed officers from the Officers School of the G.N.R.; the staff continued to grow and, thanks to the uninterrupted recovery of armored vehicles, at the end of the war it reached the consistency of no less than four Companies, in addition to a unit seconded to the General Command of the GNR, a reinforcement to the Battalion "M "Venezia Giulia", a Training Company in Milan, a 75/27 Cannon Battery and numerous Services. Many of the volunteers who flocked to the Republican Armed Forces specifically asked to join the ranks of the Group, preferring it to the Republican National Army Divisions. Lieutenant Savoia, who owned farmland in the Mantua area, made available the products of his funds to provide for the Group's food needs.

In July 1944 a Detachment was deployed between Parma, Piacenza and the Trebbia Valley, not only to preserve the area from the attacks of the partisans, but above all to guard the oil wells of the AGIP of Montechino, which provided precious fuel, unique in Italy. The crude oil taken from the wells was transported by motor vehicles in 200-liter drums. After a stop in Piacenza the motorized column, at night, in order to avoid air strikes, on pontoons prepared by the Wehrmacht Genius Pioneer crossed the Po to reach Milan, where the Oleoblitz refinery proceeded with the distillation of crude oil. Part of the fuel remained at the "Leonessa", in such as to ensure the functioning of the motorcycles vehicles supplied to the Group. The rest went to the Wehrmacht and the Italian Armed Forces.

On July 25th, 1944, a large parade of the Republican National Guard was held in the streets of the centre of Milan, on the occasion of the first anniversary of the "coup d'état" with which Mussolini was deposed: the "Leonessa" sent a special Company from Turin to attend the ceremony. On this occasion, General Ricci handed over the fighting flag to the "Leonessa" before the parade: the "M" Armored Group "Leonessa" was thus the only armored department of the Italian Social Republic to receive a war banner, consisting of a tricolor loaded by the republican eagle with lictory beam between the claws.

In Piedmont meanwhile anti-partisan actions and patrol activity continued unabated until the end of the conflict, also in support to other units of the Republican Armed Forces. In August the "Leonessa" actively participated in a vast operation that led to the re-occupation of Valle d'Aosta, which remained isolated for a few months. Eight TL37 artillery tractors were found in the basement of a large hotel in Saint Vincent, with which a Light Motorized Artillery Battery was set up.

Commander Swich was much loved by his legionaries, he aroused in everyone sympathy and security, with his natural cordiality. The Lieutenant Colonel repeatedly visited all the units of the "Leonessa", even the smallest principals, accompanied by a small escort, composed of the motorcyclist Valeriano Baccinelli, the driver Albino Medagola and the faithful officer in charge, Lieutenant Domenico Lena. The selection, both physical and political, was extremely scrupulous and only those who proved capable and disciplined could remain in the Group; the ration was the same for both officers and legionaries. Those who did not have a driving license for armored vehicles followed a short course on both vehicles and armored vehicles, before being assigned to the definitive department.

In the second half of 1944 the need was felt to have a Detachment also in Milan and in December a Training Company and a subsidiary Workshop were organized for the restoration of the armored vehicles recovered in the Lombard city. If only occasionally the Milan Detachment was employed in public order tasks in the city, instead it was his constant effort, together with the "Leonessa" departments of Turin, to guarantee the safety of the vehicle colons, who transported food to the two big cities. An efficient fuel depot was organized in the Lombard capital with an attached fuel assignment service to the various departments of the "Leonessa".

In June of the same year the 3rd Company of the Group was established, which was decentralized in the Piacenza area at the beginning of 1945, together with the 4th Company, with the logistical support of the Milan Detachment. The task of these two Companies was to oversee and defend the oil extraction plants of the Upper Emilia, plants of modest capacity, but fundamental for the fuel needs of the Group.

On 6th December 1944 the Tanks Group "Leonessa" obtained the authorization to use the "M" honor badge and the department changed its name to "M" "Leonessa" Group. This is the motivation with which the badge was given to the Group: *Solid and proud, even in the most tragic periods of national life, participated in the tough struggle against outlaw gangs, testifying with heroism and with shed blood, the high sense of duty and sacrifice with which it is animated. It participated, both organically, both in union with other departments of the G.N.R., in many special police operations in the areas of Susa, Ivrea, Lake Maggiore. It suffered losses of Officers and Legionaries and obtained various rewards for the value of heroic acts performed by his members*".

On December 18th Mussolini visited the "Medici" barracks of the Republican National Guard, during his three "Milanese days", reviewing a unit of the "Leonessa" deployed in the courtyard of the barracks. The "Leonessa" continued to carry out the tasks assigned in Piedmont, Lombardy and Emilia for all the first months of 1945, even when by now the Allies were preparing to spread in the Po Valley. Meanwhile, the General Command of G.N.R. developed an operational plan to deal with the coming days of the final attack. The provisions were issued in early April to the Regional Inspectorates and Provincial Commands, through a confidential letter from General Nicchiarelli, Chief of Staff of the G.N.R., with the subject "Zeta Requirement". The one received from the "Leonessa" Command had the following content: *"The eventual withdrawal movement, when started, must be conducted on the established itinerary and subsequently continued, without stopping, up to Lecco to end in Valtellina. In Lecco you have to make arrangements with the local headquarters of G.N.R. which will indicate the location to reach. If sudden and unforeseeable emergencies make it difficult or impossible to retreat on the already planned itinerary, you can make the changes that the contingent situation will impose or advise on the prescribed routes. The essential thing is to reach the maximum number of men and the greatest possible amount of material (especially ammunition and food), the Valtellina. To achieve this essential purpose, you will have to act with maximum energy. Since it is not possible to foresee the eventual course of events and the development of the situation that could prevent me from giving you the necessary provisions, I agree, with regard to the above, the indispensable freedom of action. The instructions imparted at the time regarding the methods of withdrawal (A - timely; B - sudden) remain the same"*.

At the time of the partisan insurrection, all the units of "Leonessa", wherever they were displaced, followed the orders given by the General Command and tried to fall back neatly into the Valtellina, even though they were unable to complete this purpose by precipitating events. The Piacenza's Detachment, before leaving the Emilian city, contrasted with an M14 tank and three self-propelled 47/32 L40, the American avant-garde that on April 25th attempted to enter the city; Lieutenant Rinetti, who commanded the platoon of armored vehicles, lost his life to save his comrades during a clash that lasted for hours. The rest of the Detachment was able to cross the river Po on the evening of April 27th and surrendered to Cassano d'Adda (MI) to the Americans on the 30th. The Milan's Detachment constituted the vanguard of the column that reached Como in the morning of the 26th with the aim of reaching the Valtellina but ended up in the hands of the partisans. Even the Battery of Bergamo tried to take itself to Como, but on the evening of April 26th it had to be divided into two columns, the first of which sustained a hard fight on the outskirts of Lecco, on Como's Lake, at the end of which the fascist officers were passed for weapons. The second column surrendered instead on the evening of 27th April in Cisano Bergamasco (BG). The unit in Turin remained in position in the city until the evening of April 28th, when the republican units of the city, reunited in column, marched towards Chivasso. In Strambino Romano, near Ivrea, the fascists barricaded themselves waiting for the Allies, who arrived only on 5th May, who were given prisoners, after receiving the honor of arms. Thus, ended the brief but intense history of the Armored Group "M" "Leonessa", which lamented 52 fallen, the last of whom was assassinated on return from prison in Pinerolo in February 1946.

▲ After the fall of Mussolini, the soldiers of the Armored Division "M" were replaced the bundles on the collar with the royal stars and were distributed gray sachets instead of the black fezzes. These changes are evident in this image, taken a few days after the Armistice, when the Divisions of the Division encountered the first German units, to which they had to return the armored vehicles received from the German authorities (BA).

▲ The two tanks arranged on the two sides of Palazzo Wedekind, the Roman seat of the reconstituted Fascist Party, under the eyes of a small crowd of onlookers (Crippa).

▼ Next to one of the two tanks there is also a FIAT 626NM, re-used by the soldiers of the "Leonessa" and a civilian vehicle designed to run on gas (Crippa).

▲ The tanks belonged to the 3rd Armored Regiment and had arrived in Rome shortly before the Armistice to arm the IX Battalion Carri in reconstitution, at the depot of the 4th Armored Regiment (Crippa).

▲ The Leonessa's tank patrol was also completed by a disarmed Desert 43 model light truck, a vehicle built in few specimens before the Armistice. In all likelihood, even the latter had been taken from the Forte Tiburtino deposit (Crippa).

▼ Chief of an AB41 of the "Leonessa" Armored Group in the first months of the department's life. The soldier still wears the old Militia uniform with lapel bands (in this case even a Saharan jacket) and on the helmet he painted the skull with crossbones, frieze of the unit (Tallillo).

▲ Some legionaries of the "Leonessa" stand guard at the entrance of the Palace. The non-commissioned officer wears the gray-green uniform of the dissolved Militia, while the tank crews carry, over the combination of blue cloth for the crews of tanks, an officer belt with a shoulder strap. On the chest of the suit, made absolutely out of order, they have the ribbons of the decorations and as frieze of the black bags they have the red "M" (Crippa).

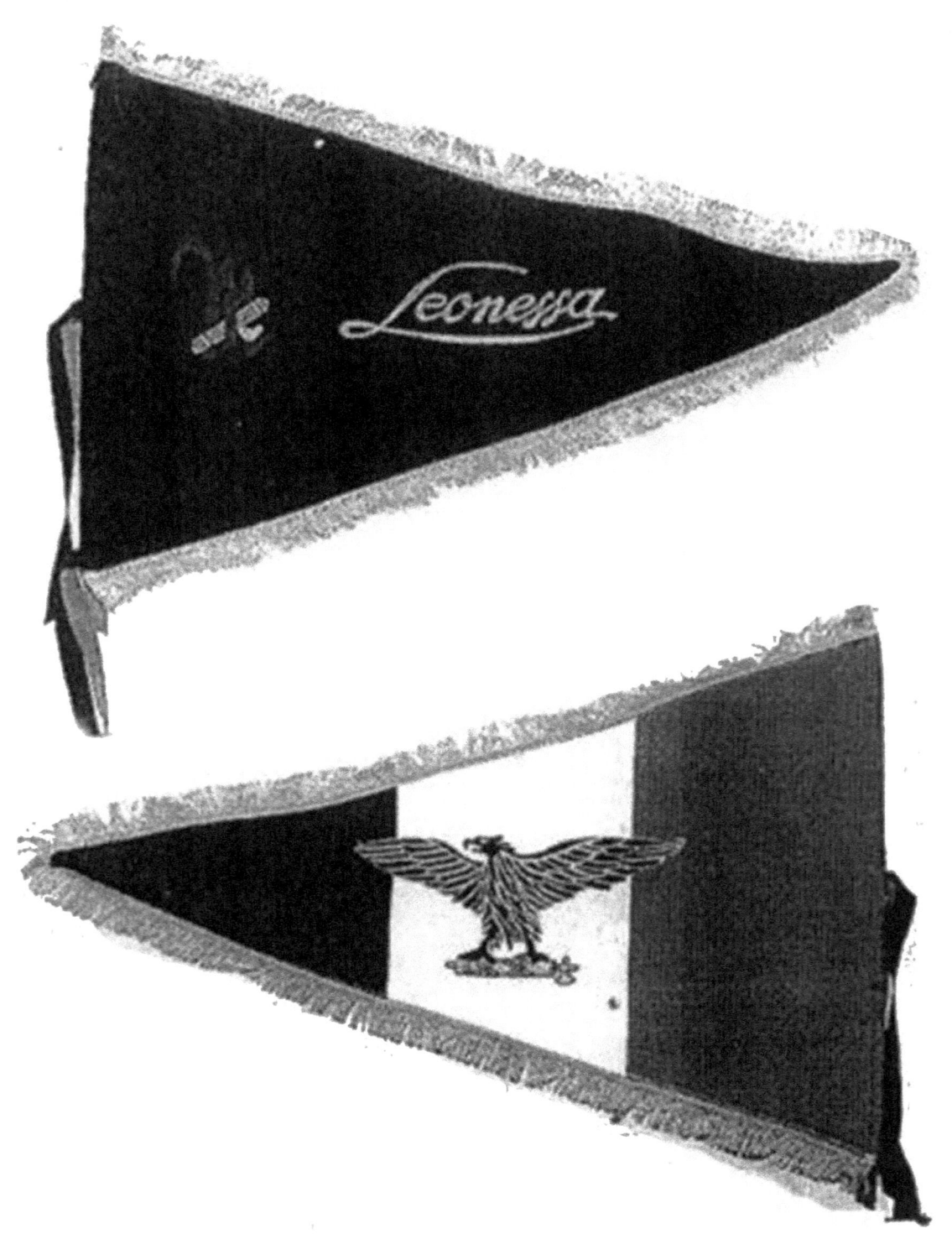

▲ The pennant of the "Leonessa" Armored Group, donated by the fascist women of Montichiari to the Group before leaving for Turin (Borgatti).

▲ The highly decorated Lieutenant Colonel Priamo Swich, commander of the Armored Group "M" "Leonessa", here still in the uniform of the dissolved M.V.S.N. (Borgatti).

▲ Lieutenant Morandi of the "Leonessa" with the crew of his tank: they all wear the new dark blue cut similar to that of the German tankmen (Borgatti).

▲ An M13/40 tank of the Armored Group "Leonessa" in anti-partisan action in the summer of 1944, probably in the Piedmont countryside. The vehicle appears painted in yellow sand (Borgatti).

▼ An armored car AB41 of the Group "Leonessa" photographed during the same operation as the previous image, in the summer of 1944 (Borgatti).

▲ Close up of Lieutenant Morandi on the tower of his M13/40 (Borgatti).

◄ The "Leonessa" also published its own periodical "Noi della Leonessa" ("People of Leonessa"), in which articles were published concerning the activities of the Group, personal anecdotes and captivating advertising pages, which incited voluntary recruitment to the unit (Crippa).

▲ L3 tank of the Legionary Gavarini photographed in the area of operations. The use of out-of-order camouflage garments by both tank drivers is very interesting (Borgatti).

▲ This "Leonessa" tank appears to be heavily camouflaged, but the red "M" still stands out on the turret, which was often covered by camouflage dyes on other vehicles. The image was therefore taken after the autumn of 1944 (Borgatti).

"LEONESSA" UNITS

1st and 2nd Companies

The first two Companies of the Tanks Group "Leonessa" were formed immediately after the transfer of the unit from Rome to Montichiari, on 29th September 1944. Initially, it was planned to train three companies to be included in the organic, 1st Tanks Company, 2nd Company Engineers and 3rd Motorized "Arditi" Company. As we have seen the Group suffered for several months of lack of armored vehicles and, for this reason, the 1st Company was almost immediately replaced by the 3rd Company, which thus became 1st Motorized "Arditi" Company. The latter located near Brescia for training, it was commanded by Captain Aristide Lissa, while the 2nd Company was commanded by Captain Zerbio. In Montichiari the two Companies were subjected to an intense training cycle, while the officers did their best in an intense work of recovering armored vehicles and weapons, dispersed a little everywhere because of the Armistice. In this way the Group was able to swear on February 9th, 1944 in Brescia, after having risked being disbanded for lack of tanks, to then be transferred to Turin. Here the 1st Company was stationed at the "Dogali" Barracks and the 2nd at the "Da Bormida" barracks. The city was almost below a siege, made by groups of rebels who tried to prevent the transit, both civil and military, along the main communication artery of the Piedmontese capital, the Milan-Turin motorway.

From the new Turin headquarters, the "Leonessa" was therefore almost immediately engaged in a series of anti-guerrilla actions in the Pinerolo area, where it suffered its first losses. The department had its baptism of fire on March 21st, when, on the orders of the SS General Peter Hansen, 500 men of the "Debica" Battalion of the Italian SS began a vast mopping up operation in the Lucerne Valley, against a nucleus of Garibaldini of the IV "Pisacane" Brigade. The attack was also attended by an AB41 and a medium tank of the G.N.R. Overall the operation was a success, but the "Leonessa" suffered a severe blow. During the action in the upper valley, the two armored vehicles were suddenly separated from the Italian SS soldiers, due to a landslide caused by the explosion of a mine, made to shine by a handful of lurking partisans. The vehicles were hit by a shower of hand grenades and rudimentary weapons, one of which hit the armored car, which fell into the stream below. The crew of three men lost their lives and four other legionaries and a non-commissioned officer were taken prisoner by the partisans. From this moment the armored vehicles and the men of the first two Companies of the "Leonessa" were engaged in a continuous anti-guerrilla activity in the whole Piedmont in concert with units of other units of G.N.R. Decisive was the support of the Group to ease the partisan pressure on Turin and a substantial part of the "Leonessa" allowed to force the partisan blocks that prevented access to the Valle d'Aosta and the Valle di Susa. A platoon of tanks was deployed in temporary support to the garments of the Republican National Army garrison at Fort Chaberton, along the French border; two detachments were also created, one in Moncalieri, at the former Royal Palace, and one at the R.I.V. factory of Cimena, branch of FIAT. Another important operation was carried out by a Group Training Company, which carried out roundups in the Val di Lanzo three on April 25th and May 7th, together with the 3rd Company of the 14th Regiment of the SS Polizei.

On May 23rd, the "Leonessa" Armored Group appeared for the first time in public in Turin, parading in force along a path that ran from Piazza Carlo Felice, passing through Via Roma and reaching Piazza

◄ Group photo of some "Lioness" officers, which allows us to get an overview of many of the types of uniforms used by this unit. From the left the Lieutenant Gioni, with the black uniform of German inspiration, the Captain Ruocco, promoted later Major, who still wears the officer uniform of the dissolved Militia, the Second Lieutenant Lena, also with the gray-green uniform and finally the Lieutenant Stable, with black beret and an out-of-order Saharan jacket made with Italian camouflage fabric (Venditti).

Castello, from where the Group returned to Porta Nuova station, starting point. Between May 27th and June 4th, the Armored Group "Leonessa" conducted a vast mopping up operation between the provinces of Biella and Ivrea, capturing 33 partisans and 3 former Australian prisoners, escaped imprisonment, recovering material and military clothing, delivered to the German Command of Turin. At dawn on the 28th the "Leonessa" also took part in the so-called "Hamburg" operation, a vast action against the partisans in the area at north of Turin, including Chatillon, Gressoney, Biella, Cavaglià, Caluso, Rivara, Ronco and Dondena. This operation was also attended by a company of the "Leonessa" Group, supported by two tanks and two armored cars, units of the G.N.R. of Turin and Vercelli, a company of Border's G.N.R. and a department of the "Muti" Legion stationed in Cuneo, the 15th Germanic Motorized Regiment on two Battalions, a Battalion of Polizei and 150 men of the German customs departments.

The structure on two Companies was maintained by the "Leonessa" until June 1944, when, thanks to the constant influx of men and armored vehicles, it was possible to restructure the entire Group, which was thus formed by three Companies. The tanks were concentrated in the 1st Tank Company, the armored cars and the protected vehicles in the 2nd Armored Cars Company and the personnel on foot in the 3rd Company Arditi, set up at that time.

The Companies located in Piedmont also took part in important operations in the autumn of 1944, supplying men and vehicles for the liberation of Asti and the reconquest of the Valdossola, in which a training company with 5 M tanks and a platoon of 10 AB41 armored cars participated. At the end of this operating cycle, an M13/40 tank was definitively detached with its crew at the Command of the Second Assault Cyclists Battalion "Venezia Giulia" in Baveno. The Black Brigade "Cristina" of Novara had meanwhile obtained to have in support an AB41 of the "Leonessa", which was used in numerous operations against the partisan bands.

A platoon of armored vehicles of the 1st Company (with 2 AB41) and a platoon of tanks of the 2nd Company (with three M14 tanks) contributed to the reoccupation of Alba (CN) on 2nd November 1944, in support of the Tactical Regroupings commanded by Colonel Ruta, formed by units of the Army, the Republican National Guard, the Republican Police and the Black Brigades.

The anti-partisan and escort operations to the convoys of the Turin headquarters continued unremittingly. The numerous reports made by the Commander Swich to the General Command of the G.N.R., relating to the activities carried out by the Piedmont's units, show how intense the activity carried out against the partisan gangs was, also in support of other Italian and German units and during the operations they complained also some injured and fallen. In these documents Swich minutely noted what happened every day, mentioning all the small and large, fixed and temporary, the operations they carried out, the staff and the means available. The units not involved in military tasks devoted themselves to training with weapons and followed theoretical and practical motoring lessons and on the technical subjects useful for the conduct of the war.

The Companies located in Turin participated for the last time in force in a public parade on March 23rd, 1945, on the occasion of the annual anniversary of the foundation of the Militia, through the cold and foggy streets of the Piedmont's capital. The previous day, a section of the Armored Group "M" "Leonessa" had participated, with a tank and an armored car, in a mopping up operation in the territory of Varallo Sesia in support of German departments and with another M13 / 40 raids in the territory of Gravellona Toce.

Between 6th and 9th March 1945 there was the last major clash between the forces of the R.S.I. and the Piedmontese partisan forces in the area of Cisterna d'Asti (AT). A platoon of legionaries of the 1st Company, with the support of an armored car and a protected vehicle, provided support for the Republican column, led by Major Gino Cera of the Public Order Company of G.N.R. of Turin, composed of the unitss of the R.A.P. located in Turin and Alba, a unit of the Black Brigade "Ather Capelli" of Turin, by a company of the Battalion O.P. of the Republican National Guard of Turin and of a nucleus of the Decima MAS. After hard fighting the republican forces stormed the partisan bases of Cisterna d'Asti and Santo Stefano Roero. It was precisely in this last location that the fiercest fire-fight took place between 8th and 9th March. The fascist column, which was blocked by the partisan fire just outside the village, was so composed: in the head there was an armored car of the "Leonessa" commanded by Lieutenant Fossati, followed by a truck loaded with legionaries, by a protected vehicle, commanded by the Lieutenant Berneschi and, finally, other vehicles of the other Republican military units. The vehicles were hit by a shower of bullets from the hill overlooking the road; both armored vehicles immediately responded to the fire. The leading AB41 was hit on its side and was immobilized by the explosion of a tire and many of the soldiers on board the first truck were killed, as Lieutenant Berneschi was killed, struck in the forehead while leaning out of the bulkheads of the protected vehicle at the time the vehicle leaped forward to respond to enemy fire. The self-protection was hit and caught fire; Berneschi ordered his subordinates to escape and, just as he covered the retreat with the machine gun on board, he was mowed by a gust in the chest. While the column was retreating towards the town, second lieutenant Fossati was also injured, trying to replace the damaged tire of his armored car. The column remained blocked in the inhabited area of Canale and the situation was unblocked the next morning thanks to the intervention of the Artillery Regiment of the R.A.P., left from Turin with urgency to help the column. The operation allowed to regain control of the railway lines that connected Genoa and Turin, continually threatened and disturbed by partisan attacks. The loot of weapons and ammunition stolen from the partisans was enormous.

In the Piedmontese capital the political office of the G.N.R. had become aware of the insurrectional plan of the C.L.N. as early as April 20th: the lifting had to be triggered by the G.A.P. (Partisan Actions Groups) with the support of a contingent of partisans, who was deploying a few kilometers from Turin. In the late afternoon of April 24th, Commander Swich called all the Group officers present in Turin to the barracks in Via Asti, where he announced that the C.L.N. (National Liberation Comitee) had asked him in an ultimatum for the surrender of the fascist units. As part of the emergency plan prepared by the military authorities of the city, the "Leonessa" had placed defensive positions (in via Asti, headquarters of the Provincial Command of the GNR, on some city bridges and at the Prefecture) to counteract any advance partisan. Swich visited the Group's city barracks, inviting the legionaries to calm and ordered not to open fire on the partisans, if not attacked, to avoid the shedding of fraternal blood. Throughout the night some "Leonessa" tanks patrolled the city, remained substantially quiet. On the morning of April 26th, in an almost ghost town, the partisans launched the attack and managed to occupy some crucial points, such as the town hall, the railway stations and some establishments. The reaction of the departments of the Social Republic was ready and decisive. The tanks of the "Leonessa" took part in the reoccupation of the buildings conquered by the insurgents, also foiling an assault on the Prefecture and FIAT was almost entirely taken over by a department of the Group, commanded by Colonel Cabras. The municipality was reoccupied around noon by a platoon of soldiers from the Black Brigade "Capelli", supported by two tanks of the "Leonessa", commanded by Lieutenant Stornelli. Towards evening the police barracks facing the "Cernaia" barracks were also released, where the headquarters of the "Capelli" Black Brigade was located. The attack was launched at around 6pm by a platoon of the Black Brigade, with 4 tanks, 3 armored cars and a platoon on foot of the "Leonessa". The action ended in the evening, when the door of the building was smashed by cannon tanks and the Republicans were able to reoccupy the building. The fighting in the city lasted until April 27th; the capital was still in the hands of the Republican forces, the battle was becoming more and more bloody and the attempts to stipulate a truce led by the Archbishop failed for the decisive intention of the Republicans not to surrender to the National Liberation Committee. On the bridge over the Po, near Piazza Vittorio, the "Leonessa" had placed an M13 tank, to prevent any attempted infiltration

▲ "Lioness" officers pose in front of an M13 tank parked in the courtyard of the "La Marmora" barracks in via Asti in Turin: from the left Lieutenant Lena, Lieutenant Colonel Swich, Major De Marchi, Second Lieutenant Ferrari and Lieutenant Gioni (Venditti).

into the square, while five tanks and two armored cars patrolled the city continuously, since it was feared a mass attack of the the arrival of the Anglo-Americans, to whom the fascists wanted to give up their weapons. The tank in Piazza Vittorio was attacked for the first time in the morning by a group of partisans, who struck him in the turret, without causing damage, from the window of a building with a bazooka blow. A new attack was taken in the afternoon to the tank stopped on the bridge over the Po by the same group of morning partisans. This time the armored vehicle was irreparably hit by a hand-held bomb track: the legionaries tried to react to the attack, but they had to abandon the vehicle, which by now had become unusable, when darkness fell. With the protection of an "Leonessa"a armored car, a truck of the "Capelli" Black Brigade managed to recover a group of White Flames that had barricaded themselves from the previous day at Casa Littoria and were under partisan siege, taking them to safety at the barracks "Cernaia". With the arrival of the evening the shootings increased in intensity and the armored vehicles that circulated throughout the city continuously opened fire. After a meeting between the political and military authorities of the city, it emerged that it was necessary to leave the capital to implement the directives of the "*Requirement Plan Z.2 - B - Suddenly*". In the evening the fascist wards of Turin gathered in Piazza Castello, where a column of about 5,000 men was formed, commanded by Colonel Cabras and whose protection was entrusted to the "Leonessa". The long column left the city at 1.40am on the 28th, headed for Lombardy, in compliance with the orders received, under a light drizzle. At the exit of the town the movement of the vehicles was thwarted by the fire of the light and heavy weapons of the partisans, but the response was immediate, thanks to the barrage carried out by the weapons of the armored vehicles of the "Leonessa" Group. The column passed through Chivasso and Cigliano, also suffering allied air strikes. On the way a lorry with a trailer, loaded with Fiamme Bianche and soldiers from the Black Brigade of Turin, turned over in a curve. Some of the occupants of the vehicle died in the accident and others were injured; the latter could only be taken to the hospital thanks to vehicles escorted by armored vehicles. Finally, the column reached Strambino Romano (TO); the wards, which became aware of Mussolini's death by radio, were stationed waiting for the events in a "free zone", preserved from partisan raids by checkpoints and patrols; many other retreating units from other areas of Piedmont and Val d'Aosta merged into the area, together with the 34th German Army Corps of General Schlemmer. General Adamo Rossi, military commander of the "free zone", where there were now about 15,000 people, became aware of the surrender signed by Graziani, made contact with the Allies and signed a surrender at 5.00 pm on May 5th, 1945, ten days after the partisan insurrection. Before being imprisoned in Coltano, the honor of arms was granted to the last departments of the Italian Social Republic.

▲ The same group of officers facing the M13/40: in the background, to the right, a FIAT 666 truck of the Group (Venditti).

▲ This AB41 armored car of the "Leonessa" Group backtracks during an anti-partisan operation, to offer greater protection to the crew, thanks to the presence of the engine. The image was taken in open contryard, probably near the Turin; the vehicle is painted entirely in yellow sand (Pisanò).

▼ Officers of "Leonessa" in the barracks of via Asti in Turin in the late spring of 1944 (Venditti).

▲ Deployment of L3 and M13 tank of the "Leonessa" in the courtyard of the "La Marmora" barracks in Turin; the legionaries still wear the gray-green uniform with the shortened jacket (Borgatti)..

▼ Detail of the M13/40 tanks of the "Leonessa" of the previous images (Borgatti).

▲ Close up of one of the CV33 in the previous photo. The photograph allows us to appreciate the arrangement of the red M above the machine-gun position and the wagon identification on the sides of the blockhouse (Borgatti).

▲ AS 43 Special (Armored) of the "Leonessa" Armored Group (Pignato).

▲ Curious combination of Artiglio and Libya tires on this armored car of the "Leonessa" Group, photographed in the courtyard of the "La Marmora" barracks in Turin. The photo dates back to 1944, when the vehicles were still painted in yellow sand, on which stand the red M, positioned on the front fenders and on the sides of the blockhouse; a red M was also painted on the rear hatch of the turret (Borgatti).

▲ An interesting elaboration carried out on the little AS43 truck was this protected vehicle armed with two Breda machine guns on a spherical support, one in hunting and one in retreat. The number of specimens produced, which were all used by the 2nd Company of "Leonessa", is not known (Borgatti).

▲ Another L3 of the "Lioness", photographed while being set in motion. The legionaries wear the first version of the uniform, the gray-green cloth with a short jacket and the black beret (Borgatti).

▼ AS43 Armored Car in maintenance in the courtyard of the "Lamarmora" Barracks in Turin (Borgatti

▲ The AS43 pick-up truck in the protected version of the "Leonessa" across the streets of Turin in the spring of 1944 (Arena).

▼ Colonel Giovanni Cabras, Provincial Commander of the Republican National Guard of Turin, while arriving at the place of a demonstration, in the autumn of 1944, welcomed by the deployed units, including, on the right, representatives of the "Lioness" tanks.

▲ Two M13/40 tanks of the "Leonessa" Group photographed in the courtyard of the convent of Lanzo Torinese (TO) in the summer of 1944, surrounded by officers of the G.N.R. of Rivoli.

▲ Starting from mid-October 1944, an M13/40 tank of "Leonessa", after having participated in the operations for the reconquest of the Valdossola, remained in garrison in Omegna, at the disposal of the "Venezia Giulia" Battalion of the G.N..R, remaining there until end of the war. In this photo of the beginning of 1945, some elements of the 2nd Company of the Battalion pose on board the tank whose camouflage coloring is evident (Aimone Finestra).

▲ In Santo Stefano Roero a column of the "Leonessa" Group fell into a partisan ambush on 8th March 1945. In the photograph the remains of a Group truck on which several Legionaries were killed (Crippa).

▼ The truck trailer of the "Lioness" destroyed in Santo Stefano Roero (Crippa).

▲ The armored vehicle of Lieutenant Berneschi, mowed while trying to protect his retired comrades with the machine gun. From the photo it seems quite clear that this is a Protected AS43 (Crippa).

▼ The vehicles of the Italian-German units in Strambino Romano (IV) after the surrender to the Allies. In the foreground you can see the armored vehicles of the "Leonessa" Armored Group: starting from the right, in the first row, is an M15 command tank, an M14/41, an M15/42. Behind, still from the right, M15/42 tanks and a AS43 Protected truck (Borgatti).

▲ Lieutenant Giorgio Savoia, officer of the 3rd Company, died in a clash with the partisans on January 22nd 1945 in Montechino (Borgatti).

OPERATIONAL DETACHMENT OF PIACENZA - 3rd AND 4th COMPANIES

On August 20th, 1944, a first platoon of the "Leonessa" was sent to Piacenza from Turin, commanded by Lieutenant Giovanni Ferraris. The garrison, composed essentially of personnel on foot, about fifty legionaries equipped with only two armored cars, was initially used mainly to escort convoys traveling around the province, infested by partisans, and, in particular, to accompany the transport of crude oil, produced by the vital oil extraction fields of Piacenza. At the end of summer, an M and an L6 tank also arrived in Piacenza, reinforcing the city garrison, which was participating in numerous mopping up and police actions in concert with Italian and German units. The command of the Piacenza base was taken by Captain Bodda.

In June, it was possible to form a 3rd "Arditi" Company in Turin, thanks to the influx of new legionaries, first deployed in the "Da Bormida" barracks in Turin and transferred to Milan in December. On 2nd January 1945 the 3rd Company reached the definitive headquarters of Piacenza, where it was strengthened by the Motorbikers Platoon of Lieutenant Savoia, with the function of an Exploration unit. From a report by Lieutenant Colonel Swich of 20th January we learn that a total of 7 officers and 113 legionaries were sent to Piacenza, with an M15/42 tank, an L6/40 light tank, three L3 light tanks, two AB41 armored cars, two protected vehicles, ten motorcycles, a car and two trucks. This site was chosen because Piacenza was easy to reach and a good starting point both to protect the rolling stock for Lombardy and Liguria and to defend more effectively the Emilian oil extraction plants. The 3rd Company of the "Leonessa", commanded by Lieutenant Loffredi, reached the oil zone after a roundup had been carried out by a Division of Mongol soldiers, framed in the German Armed Forces. The situation in the area remained quiet for a few days, but, around January 20th, there were the first signs of recovery of the partisan activity, which continued to engage the legionaries until April. The 3rd Company was stationed in Montechino and also lent itself to continuous counter-insurgency operations, creating numerous fixed facilities of different size, which neutralized the disturbing actions of the partisan bands.

In September 1944 the creation of the 4th Mixed Company was also arranged in Turin, later called "Mario Bonomi" from the name of the first fallen in combat of the Company. The Cmpany was initially transferred to Milan in October and to Bergamo in December. From here the 4th Company reached the 3rd Company in the Piacenza area in January, under the command of Lieutenant Cocomello and was positioned in Rallo di Rivergaro (PC), equipped only with armored cars; a group of White Flames formed the "Arditi" Platoon of the Company. In Bergamo, however, it kept the Command and a garrison department until March 31st. This Company detaches a handful of men in Busseto, already in January, led by Lieutenant Condemi, with an armored vehicle, in support of the local garrison of the Black Brigade of Parma, a detachment which returned to Rallio di Rivergaro at the end of March. In the meantime, the 3rd Company was redistributed: while the tanks and the Motorcyclists Explorers Department continued to base in Piacenza, a small unit of 38 men was sent to defend Gropparello (PC) and another at the castle of Montechino (PC).

Starting from early February, the units of the "Leonessa" based in Piacenza were employed by the Kampfgruppe "Binz" for operative use. At the end of the month the partisans launched violent attacks on the Emilian garrisons of the "Leonessa", aware of the importance covered by oil wells, whose loss would have meant the absolute lack of fuel supply for the Social Republic. The legionaries, thanks to the tireless charismatic presence of Captain Bodda and Lieutenant Loffredi, lasted strenuously until 10th March, when a battalion of the 29th Italian SS Legion managed to break the encirclement, beating the partisan bands. During the clashes the lieutenant Savoy lost his life, of which the same partisans recognized the value.

After arriving in the Piacenza area, a garrison was also set up to watch over the wells in Valleia (PC), composed by the "Arditi" Platoon of the 4th Company under the command of Vice-Brigadier Nazzari. This small nucleus was hit by a formidable attack in late February, which forced the legionaries to fall back on Gropparello at the end of February. Here was located, near the castle, a detachment of the "Leonessa", 24 men commanded by lieutenants Camaiora and Zenobi. On 25th February the castle was surrounded and besieged by partisans, armed also with an Italian 47/32 anti-tank gun, which weakened the morale of the legionaries with continuous attacks. Although the garrison was still able to hold out for several days and was awaiting a rescue column left from Piacenza, the two officers came to terms with the besiegers and inexplicably accepted the surrender at 5.30pm on 2nd March. All the legionaries were taken prisoner and the armored cars of the garrison ended up in the hands of the partisans. On 4th March the long-awaited reinforcements reached the castle of Gropparello, a Battalion of Italian SS with the support of two M tanks and an L6 of the "Leonessa", which could not help but note that the garrison had surrendered without apparent reason. Following an exchange of prisoners, the legionaries and officers of the garrison of Gropparello could return to freedom; Camaiore and Zenobi, condemned to death for cowardice against the enemy by a specially established Military Court in Montechino, were shot on April 5th, while the two captured armored vehicles were later recovered by the "Leonessa".

The Montechino oil wells suffered heavy allied air strikes in early April, also hit with phosphorus incendiary bombs. The prolonged bombing damaged the plants, which continued to operate until 19th April. That night the last shipment of crude oil left for Milan under the incessant action of enemy planes and attacks by partisan gangs. The garrisons that guarded the oil wells received the evacuation order on April 20th and in the following days the men of the detachments of the "Leonessa" returned to Piacenza on trucks that shuttled, escorted by an armored car. On April 26th in the city confusion reigned: the Allies were at the gates of the city and many units of the R.S.I. and the Wehrmacht were evacuating. The two Companies of the "Leonessa" remained in the capital instead and in the early morning a patrol of two tanks was sent southward, which was in contact with the allied avant-gardes. An M15 tank, commanded by deputy sergeant Donati, was hit by enemy fire, but the intervention of a group of legionaries of the "Debica" Battalion of the Italian SS allowed the release. A little later a platoon of four tanks, whose command had been entrusted to second lieutenant Arnaldo Rinetti, a university student just twenty years old, left the G.N.R. barracks direct to Piazza della Lupa. The four armored vehicles intercepted American troops on ahead and engaged in a furious battle. The 47mm cannons of the Italian tanks fired continuously for three hours against the enemy armored vehicles, keeping them nailed in place and allowing the Italian departments to leave the city. The clash was very hard and the young lieutenant lost his life: Rinetti's tank was in fact blocked by enemy fire and the young second lieutenant sacrificed himself for his companions. This was the last Italian tank battle against the allied World War II armored forces. The "Leonessa" had placed a garrison at the ferry on the Po, to disarm the soldiers (especially of the Black Brigades) who tried to flee the city to the north, collecting a large number of automatic weapons, Panzerfaust and incendiary bombs. Towards evening all unusable vehicles and ammunition and fuel deposits were blown up and the two Companies of the "Leonessa" left Piacenza. After spending the night and the next morning barricaded in the houses of the outskirts of the city, the troops began to cross the river Po to San Rocco al Porto (LO) in the evening of April 27th, under the guidance of Lieutenant Loffredi, with a squad of about thirty legionaries in the rearguard. Taking with him some American prisoners, the column headed north, with the intention of reaching Como. On the way there were gunfights both with the partisans and with American and Brazilian troops, in particular in Guardamiglio (LO), where the units also suffered an aerial strafing by three US aircraft P47, and in Somaglia (LO) on April 28th. The march of the column stopped, after more fighting, in the late afternoon in Trecella, near Cassaro d'Adda (MI). Here Lieutenant Loffredi treats the surrender with some American officials, probably from the 36th "Texas" Division. After a moving speech by the lieutenant, the legionaries delivered the weapons in silence. The men of the "Leonessa", taken prisoner, were first transferred to Montichiari and then to the Coltano prison camp. In the last days of the conflict two self-propelled L40 of the Piacenza detachment were aggregated to a German ward, with which they ferried the Po to Mortizza. The self-propelled, commanded by Lieutenant Giancarlo Fazioli, garrisoned the starting jetty for the whole night of April 25th. This handful of legionaries, having had to abandon the self-propelled wheel of Lieutenant Fazioli who had stopped due to a mechanical failure, reached Gorgonzola (MI), together with a group of Italian SS, where it had to surrender to the American troops.

The garrison of Montechino, commanded by Lieutenant Ferrari, who had remained in position despite the fact that the plants were no longer usable, received on April 20th the order to fall back on Piacenza. From here the men of this garrison, together with the Exploring Group of Lieutenant Elvezio Borgatti, crossed the Po on the night of April 21st and took the direction of Bergamo, where they followed the fate of the local Detachment.

▲ M15/42 tank of the Armored Group "Leonessa" probably photographed in Montechino (PC) in the first months of 1945. The medium tank, whose armor is camouflaged with streaks of dark color, has been hidden with branches, to make it less visible to any aerial reconnaissance aircraft (Lombardi).

▲ The self-propelled L40 of Lieutenant Fazioli, abandoned on the banks of the Po at dawn on 28th April, inspected with curiosity by a partisan (Borgatti).

▼ The Duce reviews a "Leonessa" training company in the "Medici" barracks in Milan on December 18th, 1944: the vehicles were all camouflaged (Borgatti).

MILANO's DETACHMENT

The Milan's detachment had logistical and support functions for the units deployed in Piacenza's area and it also was the training center for young legionaries, also carrying out tasks of public order in Milan and its province. At the end of October 1944, the "Leonessa" Training Unit was transferred from Montichiari to Milan, in the barracks of the "Savoia Cavalleria" Regiment, where the Milan's Detachment was formed, under the command of Major Egidio Zerbio. Probably the Detachment would have to form, subsequently, a new autonomous armored battalion from the Command of Turin. In fact, in the weeks following the creation of the Detachment, the 3rd Armored Company of the "Leonessa" was transferred to Milan; the Detachment was also equipped with its own Workshop and a Fuel Distribution Center. Another task of the Milan detachment was the management of the fuel supply provided, as we have seen, by the Oleoblitz refinery.

The Training Company, housed in the same barracks, was equipped with an M13/40 tank, an M14/40, two L3 and a self-propelled L40, to carry out its training tasks.

On December 18th, 1944, during his visit to the city of Milan, Mussolini visited the Detachment, giv-ing a speech to the gathered crowd, speaking from the turret of the 15/42 tank of the Vice-Brigadier Donati. For the occasion, some legionaries and four armored vehicles had been sent from Turin, which formed, with those already present in Milan, the group reviewed by Mussolini.

At the Command of the National Opera Balilla an M14/41 tank of Milan's detachment was dislocated from 2nd April 1945, led by the Legionary Michele Ruocco, son of the Major Euro Ruocco. The tank had been sent at the personal request of General Ricci, who wanted to use it to train the White Flame units that were supposed to arrive, units that never actually arrived. On the night of April 25th Ricci hastily prepared the tank, on which he boarded along with two other men, all in civilian clothes, and ordered Ruocco to head towards Olgiate Molgora (CO), with the excuse of going to fight with the Duce. In reality, the occupants of the armored vehicle were expected by a car, which disappeared during the night, after having taken them on board. On the wagon two other men in civilian clothes went and Ruocco drove to Como, as ordered by General Ricci before step away. In Lecco Ruocco joined a column of the Black Brigades, also headed towards Como, which however was forced to surrender by the partisans near Civate. The tank was later used by the partisans against the column of the "Leonessa" of the Detachment of Bergamo blocked, as we shall see, in Pescarenico.

The rest of the Milan's Detachment joined the fascist column which, at dawn on April 26th, left for Como, forming its avant-garde and rearguard; all were convinced that they could reach the "Ridotto" of the Valtellina[1]. The tanks arrived in the city of Lario lake without encountering any particular difficulties, traveling along the highway, along which signs of firearms were made by small groups of partisans stationed on the overpasses. On the way an M15 tank stopped due to a mechanical problem and, before abandoning it, the crew put it out of order definitively. Reached Como, the departments of G.N.R. concentrated themselves in the Granatieri's barracks "De Cristoforis", where, in the evening, after the communication of the surrender of the Republican National Guard signed by General Nicchiarelli, weapons were presented to the Republican tricolor, which was lowered for the last time. At that moment the prefect of Novara Vezzalini came to the barracks, wounded, urgently asking for reinforcements to defend the Duce, who was in Menaggio. Then two AB43 armored cars of the "Leonessa" departed, which the Group had "taken" by chance from the German depot of the Fiera di Milano on the evening of 25th April, commanded by the Lieutenants Dente and Morandi. The two armored cars broke through the partisan checkpoints encountered along the way, but reached Menaggio only at 2pm

---

1   The so called "Ridotto Alpino Repubblicano", also known as the Reduced of the Valtellina, was a belated project according to which to concentrate the Armed Forces of the R.S.I. in Valtellina, where the fascists were supposed to organize the final defense, in a fortified area for this purpose, of the Italian Social Republic. In reality practically no fortification work was carried out and the project remained only a utopia.

▲ At the end of the visit, Mussolini climbed on the M15/42 of the Vice-brigadier Donati (visible in the tower), to speak to the legionaries of the G.N.R. and to the crowd that had gathered. To the right of the tank the Captain Zerbio, while to the left the Lieutenant Borella of Milan's Detachment (Borgatti).

▶ In this photograph, taken from an unusual angle, we can appreciate the camouflage of this tank M15/42 of the Armored Group "Leonessa", taken up while Mussolini harangue the crowd in the "Medici" barracks in Milan (Pisani) .

the next day, after having had to queue up with the column formed by a unit of the Battalion "Honor and Combat" Battalion, by men of the Luftwaffe and the Black Brigades, with the slow armored car on Lancia 3RO truck of the Black Brigade of Lucca, where Mussolini was. The crews of the two armored cars conferred with Pavolini, commander of the Black Brigades, and with Mussolini himself, who dismissed the Legionaries, ordering them to return to Como (it was a diversionary move, since it was believed in this way to be able to make believe partisans that the Duce was on one of the armored cars). Although among the thousands of protests the tankers of the "Leonessa" obeyed, but their return to the city of Como was disturbed by attacks by partisans, who finally managed to surround the vehicles and forced the legionaries to surrender. The remaining units in Como concentrated on the day of the 27th at Villa Olmo, where they ceased their operational life.

▲ The deployment of the "Leonessa" Group vehicles consisted of armored vehicles partly from Turin for the occasion; in this image we see, from the left, two AB41s and two M tanks (Borgatti).

◄ Again, the Duce speaks from the turret of M15/ 2 of Vicebrigadier Donati; on the turret you can see the red M, symbol of the Group, and a lightning bolt, whose meaning is not known (Crippa).

BERGAMO's DETACHMENT

The Bergamo Detachment consisted of the Motorized Light Battery, armed with four 75/27 model 1911 guns, under the command of Lieutenant Giovanni Ferraris. The Battery was set up in Moncalieri (TO) between July and August 1944, when the Group received the four cannons and the relative ammunition's carts from the Arsenal of Turin. In August, during an operation in which the "Leonessa" had participated, 8 TL37 artillery tractors were recovered in Saint Vincent, used to complete the equipment of the Battery.

At the end of September the Battery was transferred to Montichiari; here, until February of '45, after a training cycle, it was then moved to Bergamo, where it formed the eponymous Detachment and where it remained awaiting employment until the end of the conflict, without ever participating in gun battles. The legionaries came, mostly, from the White Flame Training Center of Velo d'Astico, a total of just over 120 men.

At the Bergamo detachment on 21st April 1945 the department coming from Piacenza was joined, commanded by Lieutenant Ferrari and Lieutenant Borgatti. Late in the evening of April 25th the Detachment received the order to move to Como and the unit prepared for the departure, which took place only the following evening. In the morning, meanwhile, the two armored cars from Brescia, under the command of Lieutenant Morganti, and an L3 light tank from the Val Sesia, arrived together with a German column in Bergamo. One of the two armored cars was set on fire at the time of departure from Bergamo, as it was damaged and useless. After leaving Bergamo, the column of the "Leonessa" traveled very slowly, as the vehicles were overloaded and they struggled forward in the pouring rain. The Commander of the Detachment, Lieutenant Ferraris, after one of the most loaded trucks had been blocked due to the breakage of a semi-axle, decided to divide the column into two sections. The first section, with the fastest vehicles, would have preceded the rest of the column in Como, under the command of Ferraris. The second part, composed of overloaded vehicles, an armored car, a Light Battery Section with 4 TL37 tractors, two 75/27 guns and two ammunition carts, was entrusted to Lieutenant Oreste Romano, who had the support of Lieutenant Elvezio Borgatti. The nucleus of Ferraris crossed with caution the Adda on the Brivio bridge (LC), which had been damaged by an airplane bomb, and in Cisano Bergamasco (BG) the column involuntarily deviated towards Lecco, due to an error due to darkness and to the rain. The legionaries, however, hoped to be able to join, in the town of Como, with other nucleuses of the G.N.R. and of the Black Brigades, which however had been forced to leave the city already on the morning of April 26th. Before to reach the inhabited center the small column, made up of about forty men from the Exploration Department and the Light Battery, met an assault company of the Battalion "Perugia" of G.N.R., in difficulty due to breakdown of the vehicles. The approximately 120 legionaries of the "Perugia" thus joined the column of the "Leonessa", which had an L3 tank, a bus, some trucks, several motorcycles and a Section of the 75/27's Battery. Due to a fault in an artillery tractor and the persistent drizzle, the column reached the village of Pescarenico, near Lecco, around 2 am on April 27th, where it found the pass blocked by the fire of the partisans, who had now occupied the locality. The Lieutenant Ferrari of the Exploration Department was wounded in a foot and a legionary of the "Perugia" Battalion was killed; some legionaries attempted to advance in exploration, shielding themselves with the L3 tank, but they were forced to retreat. The men of the Battery also opened fire with one of their own guns, but the battle lasted for hours. In the morning the soldiers of the G.N.R. barricaded themselves in some houses, to resist to the bitter end, determined not to give in and indeed to reach Como, while Lieutenant Ferraris, also wounded, managed to force the partisan block with the small L3 tank and headed for Como in looking for reinforcements. The partisans of the 55th "Rosselli Brigade" continuously attacked the positions of the fascists with every available means, even with a train equipped with anti-aircraft guns from the nearby railway line. The

▲ Lieutenant Elvezio Borgatti, here photographed in the uniform of an officer of the G.N.R., commanded the Exploration Department (Borgatti).

legionaries strenuously defended themselves with all their weapons, until in the afternoon two Allied Dingo armored cars and the M14 tank of the "Leonessa" of the legionary Ruocco, captured, as we have seen, the day before while he supported a Black Brigade unit, arrived in Pescarenico. The three armored vehicles were initially exchanged by the legionaries for the long-awaited reinforcements from Como, but soon the vehicles opened fire, supporting with their weapons the partisan attack. The legionaries of the G.N.R. were about to run out of ammunition and at 17 o'clock of that terrible April 27th the surrender negotiations were opened, at the end of which the fascists ceased firing, leaving two dead on the field. According to the pacts stipulated, the legionaries should have received the honor of arms and should have been vacated after three days. These clauses were partly disregarded, the soldiers were imprisoned in a school in the city, after having been stripped and robbed of all personal effects, and on the morning of the 28th the prisoners risked being shot. Only the intervention of a priest from Lecco, Father Luigi Brusa, avoided the massacre of at least part of these 160 men. The officers and non-commissioned officers sacrificed themselves to save the lives of their subordinates: in the afternoon, thirteen officers and three deputy officers were shot by a platoon of partisans in the town's sports field, having endured the ravages of the crowd. The bodies of those executed remained unburied for a week, because the gravedigger of the town refused to bury the fallen fascists: the survivors of the slaughter were thus forced to perform the sad task, digging a mass grave. The surviving Legionaries were kept piled up in inhuman conditions for several days in a school room and employed in all kinds of work activities, to then be sent to prison camps. The two officers who had forced the checkpoint did not reach Como, but were blocked by some partisans along the way.

▲ In this image, on the far left, we note a detail of the AB43 with which Lieutenant Morandi attempted to meet Mussolini on 26 April 1945. The photo was taken in Como, after the armor was captured by the partisans, of opposite the Zucchi barracks, which no longer exists today, but which was then the headquarters of the Military District.

The fate of the Romano and Borgatti's column was not very different. After being distanced from the fastest nucleus, this group of the "Leonessa" could not cross the Brivio bridge, because the structure would have given way under the weight of the vehicles. The unit, then, after having taken with it a dozen soldiers of the Battalion "Perugia" remained isolated from the bulk of their department, lurked between Cisano Bergamasco and Brivio waiting for the Allies. Around noon, it was now April 27th, the communist partisans of Brivio approached the Roman second lieutenant, asking for the surrender without condition of the men of the G.N.R, which was categorically refused. The ward was still scared, because it was still well armed, and the Communists withdrew to the country. Later, representatives of the Cisano National Liberation Committee presented themselves, supported by Catholic partisans, who proposed surrender with the honor of arms. After accepting the proposed conditions, the legionaries were led to the Cisano kindergarten, to be held in waiting to be delivered to the Allies, but some of the "Leonessa" vehicles were cut off from the bulk of the group since the sudden arrival of an American column car. This group of legionaries, after being disarmed by US soldiers who did not take them prisoners, was brutally attacked by the inhabitants of the village and was interned in Bergamo prisons, from where he was sent to the Coltano prison camp.

Morganti's armored car tried to keep the connections between the two parts of the Bergamo column, but, due to darkness and bad weather, he lost the way. Stopped by a group of insurgents, Morganti managed to obtain a pass for himself and his men, while the armored car was taken to Como by the partisans themselves.

UNITS IN VALTELLINA

At the end of April 1945, a small group of armored vehicles of the Group (a light tank L6/40 and two armored car, of which at least one was an armored AS43) was detached in Valtellina, in the area of Tirano, as part of the project for the creation of the "Riotto Alpino Repubblicano. On April 27th this small detachment was involved in a fight between a fascist column made up of a thousand men of the Border's G.N.R. and of the Black Brigades, departed from Tirano (SO). The column, commanded by Major Vanna of the 2nd Battalion of the III Legion Border's G.N.R. "Vetta d'Italia", was directed towards Sondrio, with the intention of reaching Mussolini on the road to Valtellina and escorting him inside the "Ridotto". This column was completely motorized, equipped with trucks, some of which were armed with 20mm machine guns, and it was escorted by the armored vehicles of the "Leonessa". The column was blocked at the exit of Tirano by a large barrage by the partisans, stationed on the surrounding hills. During the bloody battle, which lasted several hours, the light tank served as a shield for the soldiers who tried unsuccessfully several times to approach the mountain where the partisan formations were, to force the blockade.

▲ Armored AS43 of the "Leonessa" Armored Group in the outskirts of Tirano (SO) in the last days of April 1945. The Group had deployed some armored vehicles at the end of the war, within the revered project of the Redoubt Republican Alpine (Pisanò).

▲ The "Leonessa"'s L6/40 tank posted in Valtellina taken up again during the bloody battle in Tirano against the local partisans on April 27th (Pisanò).

▲ ▼ Two other images of the furious clash of Tirano of 28th April 1945: the trucks armed with 20 mm machine-guns of the G.N.R. are portrayed, while they are under the fire of the partisan line. The photographs appear to be ruined, as Giorgio Pisanò, at the time official of the G.N.R, who took part in the battle, concealed the roll before surrender and was able to develop its content only much later (Pisanò).

STRUCTURE

At its official establishment on 30 September 1943 the Carri Group "Leonessa" had this structure, which it maintained until May 1944:

· Command Platoon
· 1st Arditi Company
· 2nd Company Guastatori
· Services

At this stage the Group had a very limited supply of armored vehicles.

Between June and September 1944 the structure varied in this way:

· Tanks Company
· Armored Cars Company
· "Arditi" Company
· Training Company
· Artillery Battery

The definitive structure was reached by the "Leonessa" from October 1944:

· Group's Command (in Turin)
  Command
  Command's Services
  Protection Unit
  Detachment in Moncalieri (TO)
  Detachment at RIV- FIAT" factory in Cimena (TO)
· 1st Company "*Aristide Lissa*" at "Dogali" barracks in Turin
· 2nd Company at "Da Bormida" barracks in Turin
· 3rd Company – Operational Detachment in Piacenza
  Gropparello's Detachment
  Montechino's Detachment
  Motorbikers Explorer Unit
· 4th Company "*Mario Bonomi*" in Rallio di Rivergaro (PC)
  Busseto's Detachment
· Milano's Detachment
  Training Company
  Ddetached Workshop
· Light Motorized Artillery Battery first in Montichiari (BS), later in Bergamo
  Command
  1st Section (with two 75/27 guns)
  2st Section (with two 75/27 guns)
  Section Shooting Unit
· Detachments in Lombardia, Piemonte ed Emilia.

In terms of staff, the "Leonessa" achieved high numbers. About 830 soldiers, 70 officers, 52 non-commissioned officers and 709 legionaries were registered in the Group; during the two years of life the department paid a high toll of blood, having 56 fallen and 46 wounded.

UNIFORM

The uniform adopted by the Armored Group "M" "Leonessa" was a true news among the tankers of the Social Republic. Quickly discarding the old uniform of the National Security Volunteer Militia, in the spring of 1944 a short gray-green cloth coat was adopted, cut just below the waist, with a covered buttonhole, two chest pockets and counter-shoulders. In place of the black fez of MVSN, a large beret of black cloth was adopted as headgear, with a metal skull with crossbones as a frieze, a symbol that was often used also on caster's helmets, although, in this case, it was generally painted white directly on the leather. In June of the same year began the distribution of a version of the same uniform in dark blue cloth, always composed of short jacket, but without collar resembling that of paratrooper, and long pants, closed at the ankle. The uniform for the officers was very similar to that of the German tanks; in black fabric, two versions were used, virtually identical in cut, but one of German production and one of Italian production.

On the tunic the red "M" Mussolini in the lapel were worn, the badges on the wrist for the officers, similar to those of the dissolved Militia, on the arm instead for the non-commissioned officers and troops. On the chest, on the left, ribbons and a pilot's license for wagons were brought; the frieze of daring was also granted, to be sewn on the left sleeve, under any grade badges, to those who had participated in at least three operations against the "rebels". The uniform was completed by the brown leather belt with holster and dagger on the left side; although it had to be distributed to all the members of the Group, the belt, which had a particular buckle with the "M", symbol of the G.N.R., was often replaced by the old belt with shoulder strap, especially by the officers.

VEHICLES

It is difficult to establish the true consistency of the fleet of the "M" "Leonessa" Group, because there are, in fact, no official documents attesting to the type and number of vehicles assigned to the department.

According to a publication published by the veterans of the Group, the "Leonessa" would have had this maximum endowment of means:

Armored vehicles

- 35 medium tanks M 13/40, M 14/41 e M15/42 (*di questi ultimi almeno due erano nella versione carro comando*)
- 6 light tanks L6/40 and self-propelled guns L40 47/32 (*maybe 1 L6/40 e 5 self-propelled gung L40*)
- 16 L3 light tanks
- 1 british armored car Dingo
- 18 AB41 armored cars
- 10 armored cars Zerbino's model
- 3 heavy armored vehicles
- 4 light armored vehicles
- 8 armored vehicles S 40 e 26

Trucks

- 60 trucks Lancia 3RO
- 25 trucks Fiat 626
- 12 trucks Fiat 634
- 13 trucks Fiat 666
- 10 trucks OM Taurus
- 9 trucks SPA e 38

▲ The Legionary Emilio Mandelli of the Armored Group "M" "Leonessa". The soldier wears a dark-colored parachute jacket with a neckless collar: the jacket is probably already born in a midnight blue cloth, as recently some specimens were found in undyed cloth. On the neck we can see the flames with two black points with the red "M", while on the chest the legionary carries a patent from the Regio Esercito out of ordinance, composed of an eagle of the Air Force with the shape of an L3 light tank between ali (Vendrame).

▲ Lieutenant Sanfelice and Captain Zerbio of the "Leonessa" Armored Group in the new dark blue uniform. Zerbio, a highly decorated officer, carries the badge of promotion for merits of war; on the left arm he has the "Ardito" badge, which during the R.S.I. was granted to those who participated in at least 3 anti-partisan operations. On the basque there are the stars of grade and a metallic skull, of the model used by the Black Brigades, different from the one with the crossbones of Lieutenant Sanfelice (Borgatti).

▲ Major Euro Ruocco, deputy commander of the "Leonessa" Group. The officer wears the new black uniform, but on the insignia instead of having the "red M", so dear to the legionaries, he wears the double silvered M-shaped metal spikes, used for a short time by the Republican National Guard (Borgatti).

▲ Group of legionaries of the "Leonessa" Group in Milan on 25th July 1944. The photograph allows us to appreciate the new dark blue uniform (note the contrast with the black shirt), the "red M" on the collar of the jacket and the skull painted on the tanker's helmets.

- · 5 trucks SPA Dovunque 41
- · 4 trucks Bianchi Miles

Cars and motorbikes
- · 48 cars (Lancia Aprilia, FIAT 1100 Libia and Russia models and Fiat 508)
- · 60 motorbikes (Gilera, Guzzi e Bianchi)

Artillery
- · 2 batteries 75/27 CK
- · 8 light tractors SPA TL37

Others
- · 8 field kitchens
- · 1 cloth's deposit
- · 2 mechanical workshops
- · 1 field hospital
- · 4 tow trucks

It is necessary to make some observations on this list, as regards the armored vehicles. The presence of 3 light armored vehicles and 4 heavy ones is mentioned, without however specifying what type of vehicle it was. It can be hypothesized that among these vehicles it is possible to count also the armored vehicles built on the frame of the AS43 truck, that is the so-called Special Car body on AS43 (or Autobindo AS43) and the vehicle protected for transporting troops, always on an AS43 chassis. Several hypotheses have been made, even in recent studies, on the armored vehicles cited in this reductionist publication, but these are obviously only a hypothesis. According to a report drafted by an official of the Group in the post-war period, the heavy armored vehicles would have been 2, made by the Military Arsenal of Turin on a heavy truck chassis (probably Lancia 3RO), equipped with revolving turret and armed with 20 mm machine gun, with side armor plating. The light armored vehicles, on the other hand, would have been open-air processing on a TL37 chassis, without armament. The same list also mentions 10 "Zerbino armored cars" and 8 "armored cars S40 and S26". While the so-called "Zerbino" could be identified with the armored AS43 (even if the number reported by veterans still seems excessive, given that the photographic and video documentation found always shows no more than two AS43 armored), the S40 and S26 are not identifiable with any Italian-made armored car. The presence of an English Dingo, who was even traced back to the North African countryside, is doubtful.

The only official document found, which reports the endowment of armored vehicles of the Group, is dated February 25th, 1945, now almost at the end of the war, and it is a reminder issued by the Army General Staff. According to this document the "Leonessa" had (the names of the vehicles are listed as they are in the original text):

- 12 armored cars
- 12 L/3
- 3 L/6
- 10 M/15
- 10 M/14 e M/13
- 30 motorbikes
- 24 self-propelled guns 75/34 being sold by the German side
- 1 battery of 75/27 guns with tractors
- an unknown number of M/13 and M/14 in repair

Compared to the list compiled by the veterans, we immediately notice the absence of the protected vehicles (also cited in some daily reports of the G.N.R.), of the Zerbino, and of the Dingo. Also in this case the two M command tanks are not mentioned, while, probably, the AS43 armored cars are counted together with the AB41s. There are no further information relating to 75/34 self-propelled guns in the course of transfer; probably these vehicles had to come from German tank hunter's units operating in Italy, which at that time were receiving the most recent Hetzer tank hunters. This assignment, however, did not occur, probably due to the precipitating of events.

At first the vehicles were painted entirely in yellow sand, but from December 1944 a camouflage made by brown and green spots was applied on the background color. The symbol of the unit was the red "M" of the Mussolini monogram, with a "fascio" and the abbreviation "GNR" in black.

GNR

Distintivo sui mezzi

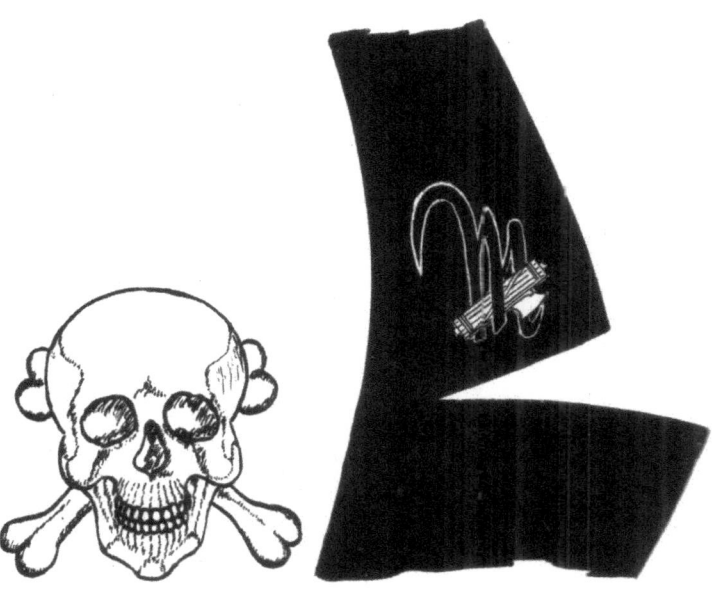

Fregio sul basco nero   **Mostrina da bavero**

▲ Drawing coming from a publication of veterans of the "M" "Leonessa" Armored Group. From the left the coat of arms painted on the Group's vehicles, the frieze used on the basques and on the helmets of tankers, the insignia carried to the collar, the famous "red M", granted only to some departments of G.N.R. (Borgatti).

▲ Vehicles of the "M" Armored Group "Leonessa" in Turin before the parade that will take them through the streets of the center. On the left the motorcycle platoon, while on the right we see the trucks of the "Arditi" Company. At the center of the image is Captain Zerbio (Borgatti).

▼ The armored cars and tanks that will close the extraction of "Leonessa" (Borgatti).

TURIN – MAY 23rd, 1944

Many of the images that we received from the Armored Group M "Leonessa" of G.N.R. refer to three important military events, in which the Group participated with its large representations. The first public release of the Group was in Turin on May 23rd, 1944, when the departments stationed in Turin paraded along a path that wound from piazza Carlo Felice, passing through via Roma and reaching piazza Castello, from where the group returned at the Porta Nuova Station, starting point. All the Group's vehicles were painted in the sand yellow monochromatic livery and only some legionaries wore the new dark cloth uniform, while most still had a gray-green uniform.

▲ Two M13/40 tanks follow the platoon of L light tanks (Borgatti)

▲ A platoon of 9 L3 light tanks opens the parade from Piazza Carlo Felice, in front of the Porta Nuova Station (Borgatti).

▼ The CV35 tank of Captain Zerbio, commander of the Platoon, taken up in Piazza Carlo Felice. On the side of the blockhouse we note that, in this case, being the tank of the Ploton commander, at the center of the black circle there is a red M with beam, instead of the progressive number indicating the tank number (Borgatti).

▲ Two AS43 armored cars of the "Leonessa", followed by an AB41 armored car of the Group, passing through piazza Carlo Felice (Borgatti).

▼ Another shot of the two M13/40s of the "Leonessa" as they cross piazza Carlo Felice (Borgatti).

▲ The platoon of 9 L3s has taken Via Roma; the commander is the only one to wear the new black uniform, similar in cut to that of the German tankers (Borgatti).

▼ The platoon of L3 tanks of the "Lioness" photographed from behind: it is interesting the lack of license plates on them (Borgatti).

▲ The M13 tanks enter Via Roma (Borgatti).

▼ Close up of the commander of the AB41 (Borgatti).

▲ M13/40s and L6/40, followed by two AB41s (Borgatti).

▲ The group of the "Leonessa" tanks in Via Roma seen from another perspective (Borgatti).

▼ The procession continues along Via Roma; you can identify, starting from the right, 2 medium tanks M13/40, a light tank L6/40, two armored cars AS43 and one AB41 (Borgatti).

▲ A FIAT 626 truck with a 20-mm Scotti machine gun in tow, followed by a Bianchi Miles of the "Arditi" Company of the "Leonessa" parade in Turin on 23rd May 1944 (Crippa).

▼ This photograph, taken in Piazza Castello allows us to appreciate the layout of the tools and the shape of the rear part of the AS43 armored car, which is clearly inspired by the prototype built on the chassis of the TL37 (Borgatti).

▲ Delivery to the Armored Group "M" "Leonessa" of the combat flag. The lieutenant Lena, with two non-commissioned officers at the sides, falls within the ranks followed by the commander Lieutenant Colonel Priamo Swich. Behind them is the deployed motorcycle platoon (Borgatti).

MILAN – JULY 25TH, 1944

On July 25th, 1944, the "Leonessa" sent a representation of the strength of a Company specifically from Turin to Milan to participate in the ceremony held on the occasion of the first anniversary of the "coup d'état" with which Mussolini was deposed. Before the great parade that crossed Piazza Duomo, General Ricci handed over the fighting flag to some of the G.N.R. fighting units, including the "Mazzarino" Paratrooper Battalion and the "Leonessa" "M" Armored Group, the only armored unit in the Italian Social Republic to receive a flag of war, consisting of a tricolor loaded by the republican eagle with a "littorio beam between the claws. The core of the "Leonessa", which participated in the parade, was composed of at least 5 M tanks, 7 L3 light tanks, 1 L6/40 light tank, 1 AS43 armored car and 1 AB41 armored car.

▲ Close up of the crew chief of an M13/40 tank. On this occasion, for the first time, all the crews of the tanks and all the legionaries of the "Leonessa" Group wore the new dark uniform.

▲ The tanks of the "Leonessa" are preparing to parade in Milan on 25th July 1944. In the center of the picture an L6/40 of the Group, on the hatch you can see the Mussolinian monogram, symbol of unity (Borgatti).

▼ M13 and an L6 tanks of the Armored Group "Leonessa" of G.N.R. on 25th July 1944 in Milan, before the parade held in the city, on the anniversary of the dismissal of Mussolini lined up at Porta Venezia (Arena).

▲ The crews of the L3 tanks of the "Leonessa" saluted while they were reviewed by General Ricci (Borgatti).

▼ The Italian and German military authorities review the units of the G.N.R. deployed before the parade (Borgatti).

▲ The Armored AS43 of the "Leonessa" Armored Group enters Piazza Duomo in Milan, during the parade on 25th July 1944, the anniversary of the Grand Council which declared Fascism lapsed. The legionaries wear the new uniform with the German cut of dark blue (Borgatti).

▼ On the L6/40 light tank in the foreground the pennant of the "Leonessa" Group flies, while on the M13 behind it has been hoisted the flag of war recently received by the hands of General Ricci (Borgatti).

▲ Legionaries of the Guard in summer uniform parade in Piazza Duomo in Milan in front of general Ricci, visible in the foreground on the right (Pisanò).

▼ Often, for speed and economy, normal trucks were used for transporting troops in action, simply equipping them with Breda submachine guns, easily moved from one vehicle to another, as in the case of this FIAT 626 NM of the "Arditi" Company of "Leonessa", photographed during the parade in Milan on 25th July 1944 (Borgatti).

▲ M13/40 tanks of the "Leonessa" Group acclaimed by the crowd in Milan on 25th July 1944 (Borgatti).

▼ A motorcyclist unit closes the "Leonessa"; in the foreground a motorbike, a widespread means of transport at the time (Crippa).

▲ An M13/40 tank enters Piazza Duomo in Milan on 25th July 1944, the front plate "GNR 4340", painted on the bow of the cart of the tank is clearly visible (Borgatti).

▲ Close up of the Sappers of the "Leonessa" as they parade for the last time through the streets of a foggy Turin on March 23th, 1945 (Borgatti).

▼ The last major parade of G.N.R. in Turin it was held on the anniversary of the foundation of the "Fasci di Combattimento". In this parade took part the men and the vehicles of the Armored Group "Leonessa", located in the city: the legionary in the foreground bears the war flag of the Group (Borgatti).

TURIN – MARCH 23ᴿᴰ, 1945

On March 23rd, 1945, the 28th anniversary of the founding of the "Fasci di Combattimento" fell. In Turin the anniversary was remembered with an impressive parade in the presence of the Republican Fascist Party secretary Alessandro Pavolini, the "Leonessa" Armored Group paraded for the last time in a foggy Turin, along with other units of the Republican National Army, of the Black Brigades and the Republican National Guard.

▲ Among the vehicles that took part in the parade on March 23th, 1945 was this AS43 armored car in the new camouflage livery, adopted by all the means of the "Leonessa".

▲ The "Leonessa" was in charge of two M15 tanks in the version for Self-Propelled Batteries Command, photographed here during the last parade in which the Group participated. The first half raises the pennant of the ward (from A. Franzolini "The Martyrdom of a People. 1943-1945", Edizioni Rievocazioni Storiche, 1952).

▼ Again the two self-propelled command wagons, on the same occasion as the previous photograph. The second half does not appear to bear departmental signs, but there is a plaque on the back, with the abbreviation "GNR", but whose number is unfortunately illegible (Borgatti).

▲ The two tanks are followed by a medium tank of the Group, probably an M14, that is camouflaged in three tones and is in turn followed by two AB41 of the Group (by A. Franzolini "The Martyrdom of a People. 1943-1945 ", Edizioni Rievocazioni Storiche, 1952).

▲ The close-up photograph of the strange vehicle protected on AS43 of the "Leonessa" allows to appreciate the dark blue uniforms of the Legionaries.

▼ Behind the armored AS43 was the AS43 "Protetta", also in the camouflage color, which partly covered the symbols of the Group, adopted in December 1944. The number plate is "GNR 438".

▲ The parade of the Armored Group "Leonessa" was closed by some trucks of the "Arditi" Company, including the latter with the plate number "GNR 4371".

PRAYER OF THE ARMORED GROUP "M" "LEONESSA"

O great Mother Italy, listen to our voices the plea we make for your glory.

Intercede for us towards that God who loves you and whom we love.

Intercede so that the strength of the "Lioness" is worthy of you, worthy of what you have given us and that you will still give us: the joy of combat.

Intercede with God so that our hearts may be armored like our weapons and beat in unison with our engines.

Make you, great Mother, that if death takes us, it has the sweetness of a human caress and that by dying we see your face serene.

Make you who from the blood of those who have fallen and if we fall, other Legionaries rise to take revenge by fighting in the battle for your glory alone.

Do you, Mother Great Italy, wash the shame of betrayal with our courage and sacrifice.

Make the traitors fall.

Make you, with the help of God, that the Tricolor of ours bound to the Republican Beam, garrese over the world in the name of immortal Rome.

So be it.

SONG OF THE ARMORED GROUP "M" "LEONESSA"

Beautiful girls, don't be sad:
you are the joy of us tank drivers!
Forward "Lioness", to the rescue
on our wagons there is the Red Emme
and turns, turns the track, roars the motor,
in iron mass there is an iron heart!

Carristi we belong to our Duce
that Italy leads to victory!
Forward "Lioness" with great ardor,
on our wagons there is the Tricolor
and turns, turns the track, roars the motor,
in iron mass there is an iron heart!

Russia, America and England,
all of us make war
but against this filthy rogue
we will vomit our machine gun
and turns, turns the track, roars the motor,
in iron mass there is an iron heart!

Rumble my little fortress,
open down to the infantryman,
next victory appears,
our brow is at the front!

Va "Leonessa" is the hour of the trial,
we are lions, we win or we die!
We are the tanks of the "Lioness":
"Iron mass, iron heart"!

No match in our exploits
of fighters, heroic deeds.
Bold tankmen, always ahead,
our motto is to win or die.

For Mussolini and for our country
we will fight and win!

BIBLIOGRAPHY

- Arena Nino, *"R.S.I. – Forze Armate della Repubblica Sociale – La guerra in Italia – 1943 – 1944 – 1945"*, Ermanno Albertelli Editore, Parma, 2002.
- Barlozzetti Ugo, Pirella Alberto, *"Mezzi dell'Esercito italiano 1935 – 1945"*, Editoriale Olimpia, Firenze, 1986.
- Borgatti Emilio, Stabile Tommaso, *"Gruppo Corazzato "M" Leonessa 1943 – 1945"*, monografia fuori commercio realizzata per i reduci del reparto.
- Cappellano Filippo, Pignato Nicola, *"Gli autoveicoli da combattimento dell'Esercito Italiano"*, volumi I e II, S.M.E. – Ufficio Storico, Roma, 2002.
- Ceva Lucio, Curami Andrea, *"La meccanizzazione dell'Esercito fino al 1943"*, S.M.E – Ufficio Storico, Roma, 1989.
- Corbatti Sergio, Nava Marco, *"Come il diamante"*, Laran Editions, Bruxelles, 2008.
- Crippa Paolo, *"I Reparti Corazzati della Repubblica Sociale Italiana 1943 -1945"*, Marvia Edizioni, Voghera (PV), 2006.
- Crippa Paolo, *"Italia 43-45 - I blindati di circostanza della guerra civile"*, Mattioli 1885, Fidenza (PR), 2014.
- Crippa Paolo, *"I mezzi corazzati italiani della guerra civile 1943-1945"*, Mattioli 1885, Fidenza (PR), 2015.
- Cristini Luca Stefano, *"Le forze armate della RSI 1943-1945*, Soldiershop 2013, Bergamo
- Cucut Carlo, *"Le Forze Armate della R.S.I. 1943 – 1945 – Forze di terra"*, G.M.T., Trento, 2005.
- Pignato Nicola, *"Motori!!! Le truppe corazzate italiane 1919 – 1994"*, GMT, Trento, 1995.
- Pignato Nicola, *"Un secolo di autoblinde in Italia"*, Mattioli 1885, Parma, 2008.
- Pisanò Giorgio, *"Gli ultimi in grigioverde"*, Edizioni F.P.E., Milano, 1967.
- Pisanò Giorgio, *"La generazione che non si è arresa"*, Edizioni F.P.E., Milano,1968.
- Pisanò Giorgio, *"Storia della Guerra Civile in Italia"*, Edizioni F.P.E., Milano, 1967.
- Podda Vincenzo, *"Morire col sole in faccia – Ridotto Alpino Repubblicano – Le Termopili del Fascismo"*, Ritter, Milano, 2005.
- Venditti Carlo, *"Domenico Lena, l'uomo e il carrista"*, Marvia Edizioni, Voghera (PV), 2012.

TITOLI PUBBLICATI - ALREADY PUBLISHING

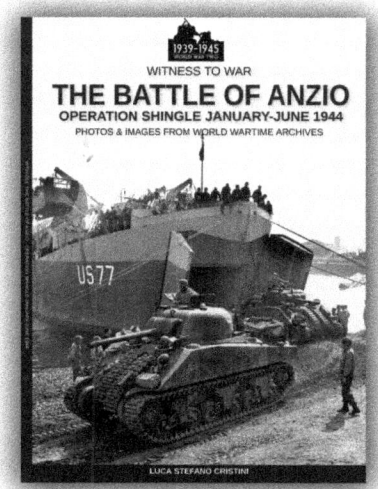

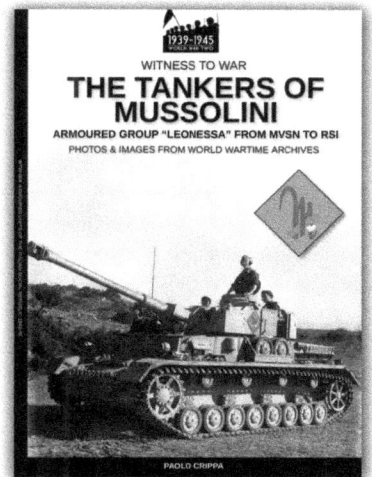

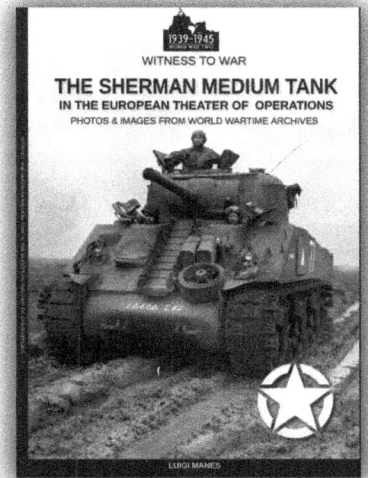

SOLDIERSHOP
PUBLISHING
BOOKS TO COLLECT